STECK-VAUGHN

TARGET
Spelling
180

Margaret Scarborough
Mary F. Brigham
Teresa A. Miller

STECK-VAUGHN
COMPANY
A Subsidiary of National Education Corporation

Table of Contents

About the Authors

Margaret M. Scarborough teaches at Elizabeth Seawell Elementary School in Chapel Hill, North Carolina. Her master's degree was conferred by the University of North Carolina. Ms. Scarborough has taught kindergarten through sixth-grade students with special learning needs. She works collaboratively with regular classroom teachers, remedial reading teachers, speech and language pathologists, and behavioral therapists. She is a member of the Learning Disabilities Association of North Carolina and past president of the Orange County Association for Children and Adults with Learning Disabilities.

Mary F. Brigham is principal of McNair Elementary School in Fort Bragg, North Carolina. She has led language arts, early childhood, and remedial reading programs for the Fort Bragg Schools, in addition to having had varied teaching experience at all levels. Ms. Brigham earned her master's degree at the University of North Carolina at Chapel Hill, where she is currently enrolled in the doctoral program in educational administration.

Teresa A. Miller has taught children in Virginia, Vermont, and North Carolina. Her degrees in education are from the College of William and Mary, and the University of North Carolina at Chapel Hill. She has worked with both children and adults in a wide variety of educational settings.

Acknowledgments
Cover Design: Sharon Golden, James Masch
Cover Illustration: Terrell Powell
Interior Design and Production: Dodson Publication Services
Illustrators: Peg Dougherty, Jimmy Longacre

Staff Credits
Executive Editor: Elizabeth Strauss
Project Editor: Chris Boyd
Project Manager: Sharon Golden

Words with *a*

a	an	can
as	at	away

A. Circle your spelling words.

1. (Can) you come to see me?

2. Don't go away.

3. I run as fast as you.

4. I ate an apple.

5. We are at school.

6. He is a boy.

B. Circle the word that is the same as the top one.

<u>as</u>	<u>can</u>	<u>an</u>	<u>at</u>	<u>away</u>
at	con	as	an	avay
an	nac	an	as	awag
(as)	cah	na	at	aawy
sa	can	at	ta	away

C. Find the missing letters. Then write the word.

1. __a__ t _____

2. _____ a n _____

3. a _____ _____ y _____

Name _____

Words with *a*

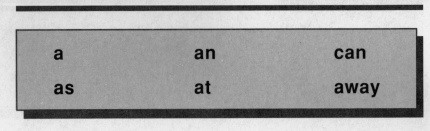

a	an	can
as	at	away

A. Fill in the boxes with the right words.

1. a n

2.

3.

4.

5.

6.

B. Fill in each blank with the right word.

1. I __can__ bat the ball.
   <small>an   can</small>

2. Are you _____ your house?
   <small>as   at</small>

3. May I have _____ apple?
   <small>at   an</small>

4. Please go _____!
   <small>can   away</small>

5. He is _____ boy.
   <small>as   a</small>

6. One is _____ tall as the other.
   <small>as   a</small>

2

Words with *a*

a	an	can
as	at	away

A. Find the hidden spelling words.

```
c  n  f  a  s  l  u  v
m  d  o  x  a  w  n  t
l  a  w  o  w  c  a  r
a  t  i  v  a  n  p  s
x  m  d  e  y  c  a  n
```

B. Fill in each blank with a spelling word.

1. You __can__ go home now.

2. Take me _____ from here!

3. She is _____ nice as her brother.

C. Use spelling words to complete the story.

Do you know what "recycle" means? It means to use

things again instead of throwing them _____. Our

dumps are filled with too much trash.

We _____ use glass jars again. We can recycle

paper and cans. _____ old shirt can be used as a rag.

Leaves that you rake can go in the garden. When we keep

some things to use again, we help the earth and its people.

Name _____

Words with *a*

a	an	can
as	at	away

A. Put an *X* on the word that is <u>not</u> the same.

1.	a	a	⊗	a	a
2.	an	in	an	an	an
3.	can	can	can	con	can
4.	as	as	as	as	aa
5.	at	at	it	at	at
6.	away	away	awag	away	away

B. Write each word three times.

1. as _____ _____ _____

2. at _____ _____ _____

3. away _____ _____ _____

4. an _____ _____ _____

5. a _____ _____ _____

6. can _____ _____ _____

C. Finish the sentences.

1. <u>Can</u> you see that _____?

2. When you went <u>away</u>, _____.

Words with -ad

bad	dad	come
mad	sad	down

A. Circle your spelling words.

1. You go down the hill.

2. Are you mad at me?

3. That is a bad car.

4. My dad plays ball with me.

5. Your face looks sad.

6. Come over to my house.

B. Circle the word that is the same as the top one.

mad	bad	sad	come	dad	down
dam	bed	sed	come	pad	bown
wad	bud	sad	cowe	dod	dowr
mab	bad	sod	came	dad	dawn
mad	bab	sap	ceme	pap	down

C. Find the missing letters. Then write the word.

1. c _____ _____ _____   _____

2. _____ o w _____   _____

3. s _____ _____   _____

Name _____

LESSON 2   Words with *-ad*

bad	dad	come
mad	sad	down

A. Fill in the boxes with the right words.

1. ☐☐☐☐   2. ☐ ☐☐   3. ☐☐ ☐

4. ☐☐ ☐   5. ☐ ☐ ☐   6. ☐ ☐ ☐

B. Fill in each blank with the right word.

1. He hit me and I am _____ .
   <u>mad   bad</u>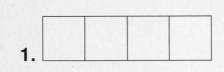

2. Will you _____ home with me?
   <u>down   come</u>

3. I love my _____ very much.
   <u>sad   dad</u>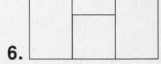

4. Go _____ the slide.
   <u>down   come</u>

5. My flew away and I am _____ .
   <u>mad   sad</u>

6. If it is not good, it is _____ .
   <u>bad   mad</u>

6

Words with -ad

bad	dad	come
mad	sad	down

A. Find the hidden spelling words.

```
a b c d a d e f
l m n o p q r s
f a c o m e t a
c d o w n b e d
v y n x p b a d
```

B. Fill in each blank with a spelling word.

1. My _____ is a good man.

2. Please _____ and see me!

3. You must go _____ the stairs.

C. Use spelling words to complete the story.

I have been in New York for two weeks. I was visiting my

friends. I _____ home today.

I don't really like to ride on planes. I hope the ride isn't

scary. I don't want any surprises. Sometimes the ride

_____ can be very bad.

My _____ will pick me up at the airport. It will be

_____ to leave my friends.

Name _____

7

Words with -ad

bad	dad	come
mad	sad	down

A. Put an *X* on the word that is <u>not</u> the same.

1. mad	mad	map	mad	mad
2. bad	bad	dad	bad	bad
3. come	came	come	come	come
4. dad	dad	pap	dad	dad
5. down	down	down	domu	down
6. sad	sad	sab	sad	sad

B. Write each word three times.

1. down _____ _____ _____

2. dad _____ _____ _____

3. come _____ _____ _____

4. sad _____ _____ _____

5. mad _____ _____ _____

6. bad _____ _____ _____

C. Finish the sentences.

1. <u>Dad</u> wants me to _____.

2. It makes me feel <u>sad</u> when _____.

8

Words with *-ag*

bag	tag	find
rag	wag	funny

A. Circle your spelling words.

1. Can you **find** my pencil?

2. A clown is **funny**.

3. Does your dog's tail **wag**?

4. I dust my desk with a **rag**.

5. My food is in that **bag**.

6. You have to **tag** him to win.

B. Circle the word that is the same as the top one.

rag	find	bag	tag	funny	wag
raq	tind	bay	tar	tunny	gaw
rab	fiud	dag	rat	fnuuy	wig
rag	find	beg	gat	fenny	wag
gar	finb	bag	tag	funny	way

C. Circle the spelling words that are hidden in the big words. Write the words on the lines.

1. wagon   wag

2. baggy _____

3. brag _____

4. stag _____

Name _____

Words with -ag

bag	tag	find
rag	wag	funny

A. Find the hidden spelling words.

```
x b c w a g m
n a p r s p o
s g h f t a g
s o c i r s t
n f u n n y e
b u m d r a g
```

B. Fill in each blank with the right word.

1. An old cloth is a _____.
   wag   rag

2. A joke can be _____.
   funny   find

3. I pack my lunch in a _____.
   tag   bag

4. If your dog is happy, his tail will _____.
   wag   rag

5. When I hide, no one can _____ me.
   find   funny

6. I had to _____ home base.
   bag   tag

Words with *-ag*

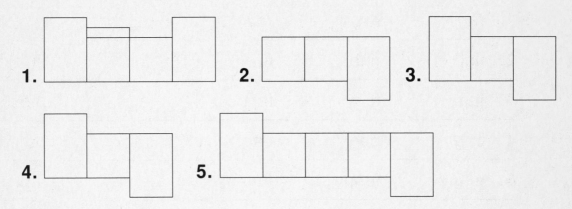

bag	tag	find
rag	wag	funny

A. Fill in the boxes with the right words.

1.

2.

3.

4.

5.

B. Find the missing letters. Then write the word.

1. f _____ _____ _____ y _____

2. f _____ _____ _____ _____

C. Draw a line from the picture to the right word.

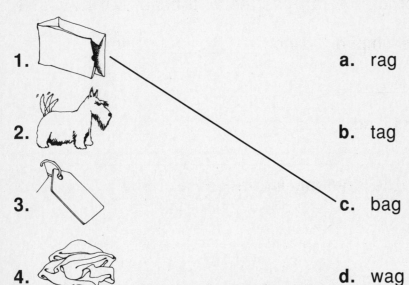

1.   **a.** rag

2.   **b.** tag

3.   **c.** bag

4.   **d.** wag

Name _____

Words with -ag

bag	tag	find
rag	wag	funny

A. Put an *X* on the word that is <u>not</u> the same.

1. rag	rag	ray	rag	rag
2. find	finb	find	find	find
3. tag	tag	tag	tag	taq
4. bag	bag	bag	dag	bag
5. funny	funny	fummy	funny	funny
6. wag	way	wag	wag	wag

B. Use spelling words to complete the story.

I love to play baseball. I'm teaching my brother how to play.

"You have to _____ each base as you run," I said.

But he forgot. He ran past second base, but he didn't

touch it. The umpire did not _____ that one bit

_____.

"You're out!" he yelled.

C. Use two of the spelling words in sentences.

1. _____

2. _____

Words with *-en*

pen	hen	he
ten	big	blue

A. Circle your spelling words.

1. A chicken can be a hen.

2. I write with a pen.

3. You have big eyes.

4. The sky is blue.

5. He is my pal.

6. The number after nine is ten.

B. Use spelling words to complete the story.

Farmer Brown had _____ white pigs. He had

one white hen. He kept them all in the same wooden

_____. It was a big pen.

_____ was afraid his hen would get lost among

the pigs. So he painted her _____.

C. Find the missing letters. Then write the word.

1. b _____ _____ _____

2. _____ _____ u e _____

3. t _____ _____ _____

Name _____

Words with *-en*

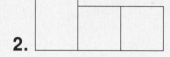

pen	hen	he
ten	big	blue

A. Fill in the boxes with the right words.

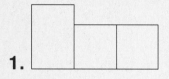
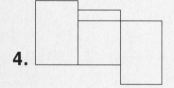

1.   2.   3.

4.   5.   6.

B. Circle the word that is the same as the top one.

<u>hen</u>	<u>big</u>	<u>he</u>	<u>pen</u>	<u>blue</u>	<u>ten</u>
hon	dig	hi	pan	dlue	net
heu	biy	ho	pen	blue	ten
hen	big	he	qen	bule	ton
yen	beg	hu	peu	blae	fen

C. Circle the spelling words that are hidden in the big words. Write the words on the lines.

1. tent _____   **2.** penny _____

3. she _____   **4.** then _____

Words with -en

pen	hen	he
ten	big	blue

A. Fill in each blank with the right word.

1. The number after nine is _____.
   _{ten   hen}

2. A chicken can be a _____.
   _{ten   hen}

3. I write with a _____.
   _{hen   pen}

4. The color of the sky is _____.
   _{big   blue}

5. _____ is my pal.
   _{He   Hen}

6. One dog is small, and the other is _____.
   _{blue   big}

B. Draw a line from the word to the right picture.

1. ten

   a.

   b.

2. hen

   c.

3. pen

Name _____

Words with *-en*

pen	hen	he
ten	big	blue

A. Put an *X* on the word that is <u>not</u> the same.

1.	he	he	be	he	he
2.	big	big	big	big	dig
3.	hen	hen	hen	ben	hen
4.	blue	dlue	blue	blue	blue
5.	ten	ten	fen	ten	ten
6.	pen	pen	qen	pen	pen

B. Write each word three times.

1. big _____ _____ _____

2. blue _____ _____ _____

3. he _____ _____ _____

4. hen _____ _____ _____

5. pen _____ _____ _____

6. ten _____ _____ _____

C. Finish the sentences.

1. I once had a <u>blue</u> _____.

2. A <u>hen</u> is _____.

Words with -et

jet	pet	help
net	wet	here

A. Circle your spelling words.

1. My cat is a pet.

2. Water will get you wet.

3. I need help to do my work.

4. The fish are in the net.

5. Let's go in here.

6. Our jet plane took off fast!

B. Circle the word that is the same as the top one.

help	jet	here	wet	pet	net
halp	get	here	met	qet	not
help	iet	hare	uet	pef	ten
helq	jet	hene	vet	pet	net
holp	qet	bere	wet	pat	vet

C. Find the missing letters. Then write the word.

1. h _____ _____ p   _____

2. _____ e r _____   _____

3. w _____ _____   _____

Name _____

Words with -et

jet   pet   help

net   wet   here

A. Fill in the boxes with the right words.

1.

2.

3.

4.

5.

6.

B. Fill in each blank with the right word.

1. The water made me all _____.
   net   wet

2. Yell when you need _____.
   help   here

3. The fire fighters use a _____ to catch people.
   jet   net

4. This cat could be your _____.
   pet   net

5. It's really hot in _____.
   help   here

6. A fast plane may be a _____.
   net   jet

18

Words with *-et*

jet	pet	help
net	wet	here

A. Find the hidden spelling words.

```
f  i  l  p  e  t  c  n
m  s  v  c  o  m  r  e
i  n  x  h  a  w  e  t
t  a  j  e  t  c  d  r
w  i  l  r  o  c  k  s
b  a  h  e  l  p  q  z
```

B. Fill in each blank with a spelling word.

1. The fast _____ got me _____ on time.

2. The man used a _____ to catch his _____.

C. Draw a line from the picture to the right word.

1. 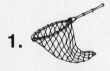   **a.** pet

2.    **b.** net

3.    **c.** jet

4.    **d.** wet

Name _____

LESSON 5

Words with -et

jet	pet	help
net	wet	here

A. **Use spelling words to complete the story.**

Dolphins are smart animals. They live in the sea. They need to be _____ all the time. Dolphins love to swim and play. They like to jump above the water. They should not be someone's _____.

Dolphins swim above groups of tuna. Sometimes a dolphin swims into a _____ meant to catch tuna. If the dolphin doesn't get _____ soon, it will die.

B. **Write the spelling words in ABC order.**

1. _____ 2. _____ 3. _____

4. _____ 5. _____ 6. _____

C. **Write each word three times.**

1. pet _____ _____ _____

2. help _____ _____ _____

3. wet _____ _____ _____

4. here _____ _____ _____

5. net _____ _____ _____

20

Words with *-ack*

pack	sack	jump
rack	tack	little

A. Circle your spelling words.

1. I have a little brother.

2. A bag can also be a sack.

3. Tack your work up on the board.

4. Jump up and shout!

5. Hang your coat on the rack.

6. Pack your clothes for the trip.

B. Circle the word that is the same as the top one.

little	pack	jump	sack	tack	rack
liffle	qack	jamp	sock	fack	nack
little	peck	jump	sach	tack	rock
lettli	gack	gump	sack	tuck	rack
littel	pack	iump	aack	tach	nock

C. Find the missing letters. Then write the word.

1. l ____ ____ ____ l e   _____

2. ____ ____ m p   _____

3. t ____ ____ ____   _____

Name _____   **21**

LESSON 6

Words with -ack

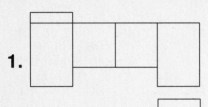

pack	sack	jump
rack	tack	little

A. Fill in the boxes with the right words.

1.

2.

3.

4.

B. Fill in each blank with the right word.

1. Please _____ your clothes in the bag.

   pack   rack

2. A paper bag is called a _____.

   sack   tack

3. A baby is a _____ person.

   little   jump

4. Do not _____ on my chair.

   little   jump

5. Hang your shirt on the _____.

   pack   rack

6. Ouch! I sat on a _____!

   sack   tack

22

Words with *-ack*

pack	sack	jump
rack	tack	little

A. Use spelling words to complete the story.

I put a _____ on my teacher's chair. It made her

_____ when she sat on it. Wow! Was she ever mad!

She made me _____ my books and take my coat

from the _____. I'm in the office now. I'll say I'm

sorry if she ever lets me back in the room.

B. Write the spelling words in ABC order.

1. _____   2. _____   3. _____

4. _____   5. _____   6. _____

C. Draw a line from the word to the right picture.

1. tack   a.

2. jump   b.

3. little   c.

4. sack   d.

Name _____

LESSON 6

Words with -ack

pack	sack	jump
rack	tack	little

A. Put an *X* on the word that is <u>not</u> the same.

1.	rack	rack	rach	rack	rack
2.	jump	jump	jump	jump	jumq
3.	sack	sach	sack	sack	sack
4.	tack	tack	toch	tack	tack
5.	little	little	little	liffle	little
6.	pack	pack	pack	pack	back

B. Write each word three times.

1. pack _____ _____ _____

2. rack _____ _____ _____

3. jump _____ _____ _____

4. little _____ _____ _____

5. sack _____ _____ _____

6. tack _____ _____ _____

C. Finish the sentences.

1. She will <u>jump</u> _____.

2. I had a <u>little</u> _____.

Words with -ick

kick	sick	look
pick	tick	make

A. Circle your spelling words.

1. Look up into the sky.

2. Too much candy made me sick.

3. Do you know how to make money?

4. A tick can bite a dog.

5. Which apples did you pick?

6. How far can you kick the ball?

B. Circle the word that is the same as the top one.

make	pick	look	sick	tick	kick
nake	qick	leek	sack	fick	klick
made	pick	kool	sick	tcik	keck
make	pikc	kook	sock	tick	kick
meke	bick	look	siok	teck	hich

C. Find the missing letters. Then write the word.

1. l _____ _____ k   _____

2. m a _____ _____   _____

3. t _____ _____ _____   _____

Name _____   **25**

© 1991 Steck-Vaughn Company. Target 180

Words with *-ick*

kick	sick	look
pick	tick	make

A. Fill in the boxes with the right words.

1.

2.

3.

4.

B. Fill in each blank with the right word.

1. I found a _____ on my dog.
   tick   kick

2. Do you _____ at television?
   make   look

3. Please _____ your bed.
   make   look

4. _____ the ball up the hill.
   Pick   Kick

5. Which color did you _____?
   sick   pick

6. My head hurts and I feel _____.
   sick   pick

26

Words with *-ick*

kick	sick	look
pick	tick	make

A. **Use spelling words to complete the story.**

A _____ is a little black bug. It likes to get on people and pets. Have you ever seen a dog scratching his fur? He might have a tick. Check yourself for ticks after you have been in the woods. If one gets on you, _____ it off. Some tick bites can make you _____.

B. **Write the spelling words in ABC order.**

1. _____ 2. _____ 3. _____

4. _____ 5. _____ 6. _____

C. **Draw a line from the picture to the right word.**

1.    **a.** kick

2.    **b.** sick

3.    **c.** make

4.    **d.** look

Name _____

27

Words with -ick

kick	sick	look
pick	tick	make

A. Write these words from the last lesson.

1. pack _____
2. sack _____
3. rack _____
4. little _____
5. tack _____
6. jump _____

B. Fill in each blank with a spelling word.

1. I can _____ the ball far.

2. _____ at me run.

3. He was _____ from all the candy.

4. Can you _____ a paper jet?

C. Write each word three times.

1. kick _____ _____ _____
2. pick _____ _____ _____
3. look _____ _____ _____
4. make _____ _____ _____
5. sick _____ _____ _____
6. tick _____ _____ _____

Words with -ell

bell	tell	me
sell	well	my

A. Circle your spelling words.

1. Can you tell us a story?

2. The bell is going to ring.

3. You are my son.

4. The cat fell in the well.

5. Did you sell your bike?

6. She gave me a book.

B. Circle the word that is the same as the top one.

well	bell	tell	me	my	sell
well	dell	fell	me	ym	soll
wall	ball	tell	mo	mg	sall
woll	bell	llet	em	my	sell
will	pell	tall	ma	ny	lles

C. Find the missing letters. Then write the word.

1. _____ y _____

2. b _____ _____ _____ _____

3. w _____ _____ _____ _____

© 1991 Steck-Vaughn Company. Target 180

Name _____

LESSON 8   Words with *-ell*

bell	tell	me
sell	well	my

A. Fill in the boxes with the right words.

1. ☐☐   2. ☐☐☐☐   3. ☐☐☐☐

4. ☐☐☐☐   5. ☐☐☐   6. ☐☐☐☐

B. Fill in each blank with the right word.

1. Do you like _____?
   me   my

2. _____ me how to do it.
   Bell   Tell

3. I do not feel _____.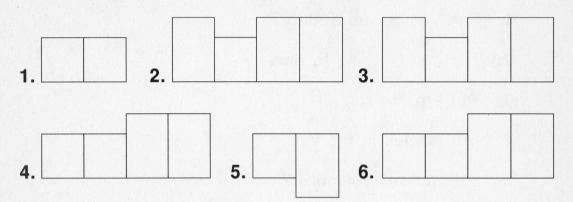
   well   sell

4. We are going to _____ our car.
   well   sell

5. The _____ is going to ring.
   bell   tell

6. Do you have _____ pencil?
   me   my

bell	tell	me
sell	well	my

A. Use spelling words to complete the story.

I saw a big _____. It is called the Liberty Bell. I

told _____ friend all about it. This bell used to ring to

_____ all of us that we are free. Now the bell has a

big crack in it. It is kept in a special place. No one will ever

_____ it, because it is an important part of our history.

B. Circle the spelling words that are hidden in the big words. Write the words on the lines.

1. belly _____

2. meet _____

3. teller _____

4. swell _____

C. Draw a line from the word to the right picture.

1. bell

2. tell

a.

3. sell

b.

4. well

c.

d.

Name _____

Words with -ell

bell	tell	me
sell	well	my

A. Put an *X* on the word that is <u>not</u> the same.

1. sell   sell   soll   sell   sell

2. me   me   me   we   me

3. tell   fell   tell   tell   tell

4. well   well   well   well   wefl

5. my   my   mg   my   my

6. bell   bell   bell   boll   bell

B. Write each word three times.

1. bell   _____   _____   _____

2. sell   _____   _____   _____

3. tell   _____   _____   _____

4. well   _____   _____   _____

5. me   _____   _____   _____

6. my   _____   _____   _____

C. Finish the sentences.

1. I will not <u>sell</u> _____.

2. <u>Tell</u> me about _____.

Words with -*ill*

ill	hill	not
fill	pill	one

A. Circle your spelling words.

1. They went up the hill.

2. You are one of my best friends.

3. Do not say that!

4. Fill the bucket with water.

5. If you are ill, you are sick.

6. The doctor said to take a pill.

B. Circle the word that is the same as the top one.

fill	ill	pill	hill	not	one
till	lil	pell	kill	ton	eon
fell	lli	qill	bill	not	neo
fill	ill	pill	hill	nat	oen
tell	ell	bill	rill	tan	one

C. Find the missing letters. Then write the word.

1. _____ n _____   _____

2. i _____ _____   _____

3. p _____ _____ _____   _____

Name _____

Words with *-ill*

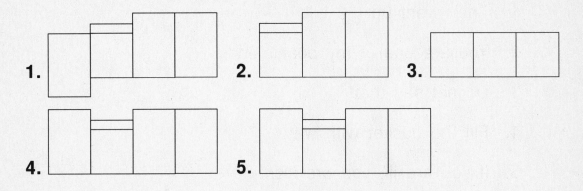

ill	hill	not
fill	pill	one

A. Fill in the boxes with the right words.

1.
2.
3.

4.
5.

B. Fill in each blank with the right word.

1. I can _____ the pail.
   fill   hill

2. You did _____ do it, so I did.
   not   one

3. Take this _____ with water.
   hill   pill

4. We went up the _____.
   fill   hill

5. I have only _____ pen.
   one   not

6. If you are sick, you are _____.
   fill   ill

34

Words with -*ill*

ill	hill	not
fill	pill	one

A. Find the hidden spelling words.

```
r  j  f  p  g  c  l  b
v  a  i  i  r  d  m  c
s  h  l  l  n  o  t  x
t  i  l  l  e  n  p  z
a  h  i  l  l  e  g  k
j  r  d  q  n  o  w  y
```

B. Circle the spelling words that are hidden in the big words. Write the words on the lines.

1. hilly _____

2. knot _____

3. spill _____

4. till _____

C. Write a spelling word under each picture.

1. _____

2. _____

3. _____

D. Write these words from lessons before.

1. away _____

2. down _____

3. blue _____

4. pack _____

Name _____

Words with -ill

ill	hill	not
fill	pill	one

A. Use spelling words to complete the story.

A nest of ants is called an ant _____. The nest has lots of small rooms. Many workers and _____ queen live in an ant hill.

The workers are busy all the time. They _____ the rooms with food. They keep the nest clean. The workers also take care of the young ants. The queen does _____ work. Her only job is to lay the eggs.

B. Write each word three times.

1. ill _____ _____ _____

2. pill _____ _____ _____

3. hill _____ _____ _____

4. not _____ _____ _____

C. Finish the sentences.

1. When I am i̱ḻl, _____.

2. The hi̱ll was as big as _____.

3. I am no̱t _____.

Words with *-ock*

rock	dock	play
sock	lock	red

A. Circle your spelling words.

1. Lock the door as you leave.

2. Some apples are red.

3. I put on my sock.

4. I fell down on a big rock.

5. The boat pulled up to the dock.

6. Let's play that game.

B. Circle the word that is the same as the top one.

dock	rock	play	red	lock	sock
bock	nock	qlay	der	lack	sock
dock	reck	play	rod	lock	stock
deck	rock	plya	red	luck	sack
qock	roch	blay	ned	loch	soch

C. Find the missing letters. Then write the word.

1. p _____ _____ y   _____

2. d _____ _____ _____   _____

3. _____ e d   _____

Name _____

Words with *-ock*

| rock | dock | play |
| sock | lock | red |

A. Fill in the boxes with the right words.

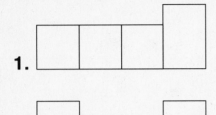

1.

2.

3.

4.

B. Fill in each blank with the right word.

1. The boat pulled up to the _____.
   dock   sock

2. The door needs a _____ on it.
   rock   lock

3. I took off my shoe and _____.
   dock   sock

4. My gum is as hard as a _____.
   rock   sock

5. Do you ever _____ cards?
   red   play

6. The fire truck is the color _____.
   red   play

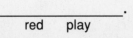

Words with -ock

rock	dock	play
sock	lock	red

A. Find the hidden spelling words.

```
l o c k r o c k
a c k o o m o p
y s s o c k e y
m z p t d o c k
e h l v e r e n
n s a c d e n a
o c y u v d t p
```

B. Write a spelling word under each picture.

1. _____ 2. _____ 3. _____

C. Fill in each blank with a spelling word.

1. We put a _____ on the door to keep people out.

2. If your foot is cold, put on a _____.

3. I like to fish off the _____.

4. She picked up the heavy _____.

5. We like to _____ in the snow.

Name _____

LESSON 10   Words with -ock

rock	dock	play
sock	lock	red

A. Put an *X* on the word that is <u>not</u> the same.

1.	lock	lock	look	lock	lock
2.	play	play	plag	play	play
3.	dock	doch	dock	dock	dock
4.	sock	sock	sock	sock	soek
5.	rock	rock	roch	rock	rock
6.	red	red	rod	red	red

B. Use spelling words to complete the story.

We live by a big lake. There is a _____ near our house. I like to _____ there. Sometimes I jump off the dock and swim in the water.

One day I jumped in the lake with my shoes on. They came off, but I found them. I lost just one _____. It was white and _____.

C. Use two of the spelling words in sentences.

1. _____

2. _____

40

Words with -ess

mess	came	said
less	run	see

A. Circle your spelling words.

1. I can see things that are far away.

2. We came home after school.

3. What a mess you made on the table!

4. Don't run in the hall at school.

5. Did you hear what I said?

6. Five is less than six.

B. Circle the word that is the same as the top one.

mess	said	run	came	less	see
ness	saib	nur	come	lass	ese
wess	said	rnu	coma	less	sse
mess	siad	run	cawe	lses	see
mees	ssid	nun	came	leas	ees

C. Find the missing letters. Then write the word.

1. s _____ _____ _____   _____

2. m _____ _____ _____   _____

3. _____ e e   _____

Name _____

© 1991 Steck-Vaughn Company. Target 180

Words with *-ess*

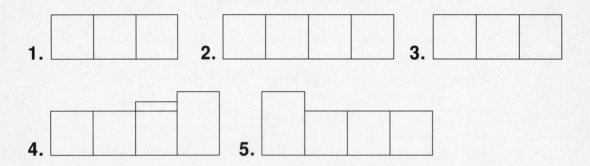

mess	came	said
less	run	see

A. Fill in the boxes with the right words.

1. ☐☐☐

2. ☐☐☐☐

3. ☐☐☐

4. ☐☐☐☐

5. ☐☐☐☐

B. Fill in each blank with the right word.

1. I can _____ and jump.
   _{run   less}

2. This glass has _____ water than that one.
   _{run   less}

3. I did not hear what you _____.
   _{said   see}

4. The girl _____ to play.
   _{came   mess}

5. I dropped my milk and made a _____.
   _{mess   less}

6. You _____ with your eyes.
   _{run   see}

Words with -ess

mess	came	said
less	run	see

A. Use spelling words to complete the story.

I _____ to see the softball game. It was the Bears

against the Jays. My friends play for the Jays. Our team could

not _____ or hit as well as the Bears. You could tell

we had practiced _____ than the other team. I didn't

want to _____ the Jays lose, so I went home.

B. Circle the spelling words that are hidden in the big words.
Write the words on the lines.

1. messy _____   2. seed _____

3. runt _____   4. lesson _____

C. Draw a line from the word to the right picture.

1. run   **a.**

2. see   **b.**

3. mess   **c.**

4. said   **d.**

Name _____   **43**

Words with -ess

mess	came	said
less	run	see

A. Write these words from lessons before.

1. pill _____   2. one _____

3. red _____   4. dock _____

5. lock _____   6. rock _____

B. Fill in each blank with a spelling word.

1. Three is _____ than four.

2. The house is a _____.

3. Did you _____ my work?

4. She _____ to see me.

C. Write each word three times.

1. run _____ _____ _____

2. came _____ _____ _____

3. less _____ _____ _____

4. mess _____ _____ _____

5. see _____ _____ _____

6. said _____ _____ _____

Words with *-amp*

camp	lamp	you
damp	ramp	we

A. Circle your spelling words.

1. When a mop is damp, it is wet.

2. Push the cart up the ramp.

3. You are a good friend.

4. I went away to a camp.

5. A lamp gives off light.

6. We all want to eat lunch.

B. Circle the word that is the same as the top one.

ramp	lamp	we	camp	you	damp
namp	lump	we	capm	yon	pamd
rump	lomp	me	comp	yuo	domp
ramp	plam	ve	cump	you	demp
ramq	lamp	wo	camp	yeu	damp

C. Find the missing letters. Then write the word.

1. c _____ _____ _____   _____

2. _____ o _____   _____

3. l _____ _____ _____   _____

Name _____

Words with -*amp*

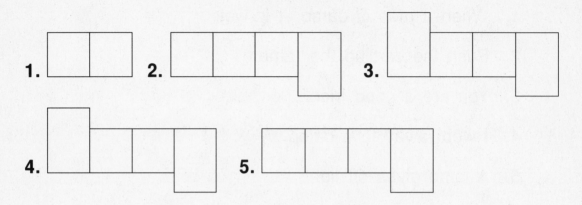

| camp | lamp | you |
| damp | ramp | we |

A. Fill in the boxes with the right words.

1.
2.
3.

4.
5.

B. Fill in each blank with the right word.

1. My hair is still _____.

damp   camp

2. Push the cart up the _____.

lamp   ramp

3. Do _____ like TV?

you   ramp

4. The _____ will not come on.

ramp   lamp

5. We put up a tent at _____.

camp   damp

6. 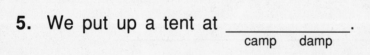 _____ will have soup for lunch.

We   Lamp

46

Words with -amp

camp	lamp	you
damp	ramp	we

A. Find the hidden spelling words.

```
e  l  m  r  u  v  c  d
s  a  w  e  c  a  d  c
t  m  y  s  i  n  a  a
w  p  o  t  u  m  m  m
b  f  u  r  a  m  p  p
```

B. Write the spelling words in ABC order.

1. _____   2. _____   3. _____

4. _____   5. _____   6. _____

C. Use spelling words to complete the story.

Last summer I went to _____ at a lake.

_____ learned how to do many new things. We

pushed a boat down a _____ so it could float. Our

shoes and jeans got wet when we did this. I loved to row

across the lake.

It was fun to make a big campfire. We would sit around

the fire and tell stories. In our tent, we had to use a

_____. I loved summer camp.

© 1991 Steck-Vaughn Company. Target 180

Name_____

LESSON 12   Words with -*amp*

camp	lamp	you
damp	ramp	we

A. Draw a line from the picture to the right word.

 1.   **a.** damp

 2.   **b.** lamp

 3.   **c.** camp

 4.   **d.** ramp

B. Write each word three times.

1. you   _____   _____   _____

2. ramp   _____   _____   _____

3. lamp   _____   _____   _____

4. we   _____   _____   _____

5. camp   _____   _____   _____

6. damp   _____   _____   _____

C. Finish the sentences.

1. At camp, we _____.

2. My clothes got damp when _____.

48

Words with -ump

bump	pump	three
lump	dump	two

A. Circle your spelling words.

1. One and one is two.

2. I fell down and got a bump on my head.

3. Do not dump that mess here!

4. I need an air pump for my bike tires.

5. I have three books.

6. There is a lump in my bed.

B. Circle the word that is the same as the top one.

pump	three	two	dump	lump	bump
dump	three	tow	bump	dump	lump
pumq	there	two	pump	pump	pump
pump	theer	wot	dumq	plum	bump
qump	trhee	owt	dump	lump	dump

C. Find the missing letters. Then write the word.

1. t h _____ _____ _____   _____

2. p u _____ _____   _____

3. l _____ m _____   _____

Name _____

Words with -*ump*

bump	pump	three
lump	dump	two

A. Fill in the boxes with the right words.

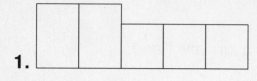

B. Fill in each blank with the right word.

1. One from four is _____.
   two   three

2. Do not _____ that mess here!
   pump   dump

3. I need an air _____ for my bike tires.
   pump   lump

4. I fell down and got a _____ on my head.
   bump   dump

5. There is a _____ in my bed.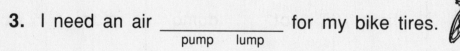
   lump   pump

6. She gave me _____ flowers.
   two   three

Words with *-ump*

bump	**pump**	**three**
lump	**dump**	**two**

A. Find the hidden spelling words.

```
l  c  n  o  p  a  f
s  o  b  b  u  x  t
f  e  l  u  m  p  h
t  w  o  m  p  e  r
d  u  m  p  n  o  e
a  i  r  m  a  s  e
```

B. Fill in each blank with a spelling word.

1. Please _____ some gas into the _____ truck.

2. The girl has _____ or _____ dollars left.

C. Use spelling words to complete the story.

Sometimes my family picnics at the state park. To get water, you must walk to a _____. You pump the water and then carry it back. You must also walk a long way to _____ your trash. It feels like _____ or three miles.

I like to go on picnics. But they are a lot of work.

"What is this _____ on my arm? Oh, no! Mosquitos!" Maybe I don't like to go on picnics.

Name _____

51

LESSON 13 Words with *-ump*

bump	pump	three
lump	dump	two

A. Draw a line from the word to the right picture.

1. bump

a.

2. lump

b.

3. dump

c.

4. pump

d.

5. three

e.

B. Write each word three times.

1. bump   _____ _____ _____

2. lump   _____ _____ _____

3. dump   _____ _____ _____

4. pump   _____ _____ _____

5. three _____ _____ _____

6. two   _____ _____ _____

52

Words with *-and*

band	sand	for
land	hand	go

A. Circle your spelling words.

1. I have a ring on my hand.

2. Do you play in the school band?

3. Will you go with me?

4. The plane will land soon.

5. Please open the door for me.

6. Sand is in my shoes.

B. Circle the word that is the same as the top one.

<u>hand</u>	<u>sand</u>	<u>for</u>	<u>land</u>	<u>band</u>	<u>go</u>
band	saud	fro	land	danb	ga
hanb	sanb	tor	laud	band	ge
haud	sand	for	lanb	bend	qo
hand	sond	far	loud	baud	go

C. Find the missing letters. Then write the word.

1. h _____ _____ _____   _____

2. b _____ _____ d   _____

3. f _____ _____   _____

© 1991 Steck-Vaughn Company. Target 180

Name _____

Words with *-and*

band	sand	for
land	hand	go

A. Fill in the boxes with the right words.

1.

2.

3.

4.

5.

B. Fill in each blank with the right word.

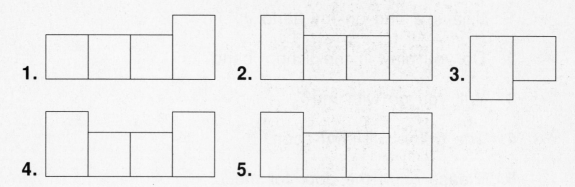

1. Do you play in the school _____?
   <u>hand   band</u>

2. Let's _____ to a movie.
   <u>for   go</u>

3. The plane is going to _____.
   <u>sand   land</u>

4. I cut my _____.
   <u>hand   land</u>

5. Get that _____ me, please.
   <u>for   go</u>

6. I have _____ in my shoe.
   <u>sand   band</u>

Words with -and

band	sand	for
land	hand	go

A. **Find the hidden spelling words.**

```
f  g  h  a  n  d  s  r
o  o  l  x  h  a  a  c
r  e  a  y  b  a  n  d
e  c  n  o  v  m  d  r
k  u  d  a  n  d  i  e
```

B. **Write the spelling words in ABC order.**

1. _____   2. _____   3. _____

4. _____   5. _____   6. _____

C. **Use spelling words to complete the story.**

I play the drums in our school _____. We went on

a band trip. Our football team was playing in a town on the

coast. We went there _____ the big game.

But first we went down to the beach. We played volleyball

in the _____. I jumped up for the ball. I fell and hurt

my _____. Now I can't play the drums. I hope I get

to play for the next game.

Name _____   **55**

Words with -and

band	sand	for
land	hand	go

A. Fill in each blank with a spelling word.

1. She plays the drums in the school _____.

2. We built a castle in the _____.

3. If you know the answer, hold up your _____.

4. Our house is on rocky _____.

B. Write a spelling word under each picture.

2.

1. _____   2. _____   3. _____

C. Write each word three times.

1. band   _____   _____   _____

2. sand   _____   _____   _____

3. hand   _____   _____   _____

4. land   _____   _____   _____

5. for   _____   _____   _____

6. go   _____   _____   _____

Words with *-end*

mend	send	where
bend	lend	yellow

A. Circle your spelling words.

1. Please send me a letter soon.

2. Where is the cat?

3. She will lend me the book.

4. The sun is yellow.

5. I will mend my sock.

6. Don't bend it too far.

B. Circle the word that is the same as the top one.

where	send	bend	yellow	mend	lend
were	seud	denb	yellov	nemd	lend
where	senb	bned	yellom	mand	lenb
wheer	sned	beud	yellow	mend	leub
wehre	send	bend	yellew	menb	lenp

C. Draw a line from the word to the right picture.

1. bend

a.

2. mend

b.

Name _____

Words with *-end*

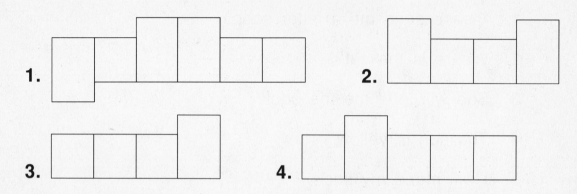

| mend | send | where |
| bend | lend | yellow |

A. Fill in the boxes with the right words.

1.

2.

3.

4.

B. Fill in each blank with the right word.

1. Please _____ me a letter soon.
   <small>send   mend</small>

2. Will you _____ me a dollar?
   <small>bend   lend</small>

3. The sun is _____.
   <small>where   yellow</small>

4. I will _____ my sock.
   <small>mend   bend</small>

5. _____ did she go?
   <small>Where   Yellow</small>

6. Please _____ your elbow.
   <small>bend   yellow</small>

58

Words with -end

mend	send	where
bend	lend	yellow

A. Find the hidden spelling words.

```
s  v  t  w  h  s  t  o
e  a  x  h  e  r  e  s
n  c  y  e  l  l  o  w
d  e  o  r  b  e  n  d
e  g  m  e  a  n  e  y
r  i  m  e  n  d  b  r
```

B. Find the missing letters. Then write the word.

1. y _____ _____ _____ o w _____

2. s _____ n _____ _____

3. m _____ _____ _____ _____

C. Write the spelling words in ABC order.

1. _____   **2.** _____   **3.** _____

4. _____   **5.** _____   **6.** _____

D. Finish the sentences.

1. Do not <u>bend</u> _____.

2. <u>Where</u> is _____?

Name _____

Words with *-end*

mend	send	where
bend	lend	yellow

A. Write these words from lessons before.

1. rock _____
2. mess _____
3. lamp _____
4. pump _____

B. Use spelling words to complete the story.

Can you _____ me some money? I want to

_____ some flowers to a friend. I think I'll send

some _____ roses.

My friend is sick. Her back hurts, and she cannot

_____ over. Thanks for the money. She will know I

care about her.

C. Write each word three times.

1. mend _____ _____ _____
2. bend _____ _____ _____
3. send _____ _____ _____
4. lend _____ _____ _____
5. yellow _____ _____ _____
6. where _____ _____ _____

Words with -ent

dent	tent	to
sent	went	up

A. Circle your spelling words.

1. We went on a boat ride.

2. She sent me a letter.

3. Are you going to school?

4. Let's walk up the steps.

5. We camp out in a tent.

6. There is a dent in my car.

B. Circle the word that is the same as the top one.

went	tent	dent	sent	to	up
went	fent	bend	sont	fo	pu
want	tant	dent	seut	te	up
weut	tent	deut	senf	to	uq
wenf	tenf	denf	sent	ta	vp

C. Draw a line from the word to the right picture.

1. tent

a.

2. up

b.

Name _____

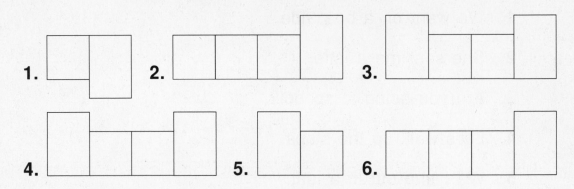

dent	tent	to
sent	went	up

A. Fill in the boxes with the right words.

1.

2.

3.

4.

5.

6.

B. Fill in each blank with the right word.

1. Let's walk _____ the steps.
   <u>tent   up</u>

2. Are you going _____ school?
   <u>up   to</u>

3. She _____ me a letter.
   <u>sent   went</u>

4. We _____ to her house.
   <u>sent   went</u>

5. Can you put up a _____?
   <u>dent   tent</u>

6. That's a big _____ in your car.
   <u>dent   went</u>

62

Words with *-ent*

dent	tent	to
sent	went	up

A. Use spelling words to complete the story.

When I was a kid, I liked _____ camp with my

mom and dad. Dad brought a _____ to sleep in.

Mom took food for us to eat.

At the camp I helped Dad put _____ the tent.

Mom cooked the food. One time we had to eat cold food.

Our pot had a _____ and a hole in it. So we ate

cold beans out of the can. They tasted funny.

B. Find the missing letters. Then write the word.

1. w e _____ _____   _____

2. s _____ _____ _____   _____

3. t _____   _____

4. _____ p   _____

C. Circle the letters that are the same in each word.

dent   sent   tent   went

The word family is _____.

The two other words in the lesson are _____ _____.

Name _____

Words with *-ent*

dent	tent	to
sent	went	up

A. Use spelling words to complete the puzzle.

Across

3. a house for camping

4. My car has a _____.

Down

1. He _____ to sleep.

2. I _____ the letter.

B. Write these words from lessons before.

1. yellow _____ **2.** land _____

3. three _____ **4.** ramp _____

C. Write each word three times.

1. dent _____ _____ _____

2. sent _____ _____ _____

3. tent _____ _____ _____

4. went _____ _____ _____

5. up _____ _____ _____

6. to _____ _____ _____

Words with -ast

cast	last	all
fast	mast	am

A. Circle your spelling words.

1. A sailboat has a mast.

2. Please give me all your help.

3. I am glad to be here.

4. Can you run fast?

5. He broke his leg and now wears a cast.

6. Were you first, second, third, or last?

B. Circle the word that is the same as the top one.

last	cast	all	mast	am	fast
lost	tasc	ell	wast	am	fast
laat	cest	oll	mast	em	fasf
lasf	cost	ull	masf	an	fost
last	cast	all	most	aw	fust

C. Find the missing letters. Then write the word.

1. l _____ _____ t   _____

2. a _____ _____   _____

3. _____ m   _____

© 1991 Steck-Vaughn Company. Target 180

Name _____

Words with -ast

cast	last	all
fast	mast	am

A. Fill in the boxes with the right words.

1.
2.
3.
4.
5.

B. Fill in each blank with the right word.

1. I broke my leg and need a _____.
   fast   cast

2. I can run _____.
   fast   cast

3. You were first, and he was _____.
   last   mast

4. We are _____ here at school.
   all   am

5. I _____ not happy.
   all   am

6. The _____ holds the sail on a boat.
   last   mast

Words with *-ast*

cast	last	all
fast	mast	am

A. **Use spelling words to complete the story.**

My friends and I race sailboats. We are very _____.

I like to win, but today I came in _____.

When I wasn't looking, my boat hit a rock. I fell into the

lake. Then the _____ hit my head. Next time, I

_____ going to watch for rocks.

B. **Fill in each blank with a spelling word.**

1. Run _____, and you will not be _____!

2. I _____ glad that my leg does not need a _____.

C. **Draw a line from the sentence to the right picture.**

1. This is a cast.

a.

2. He is fast.

b.

3. This is last.

c.

4. This is a mast.

d.

Name _____

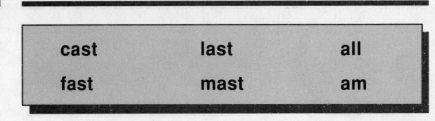

Words with -ast

cast	last	all
fast	mast	am

A. Write the spelling word that rhymes with the underlined word *and* makes sense.

1. The ship lost its <u>mast</u>,

So it could not sail very _____.

2. It can be a <u>blast</u>

To have friends sign your _____.

B. Write these words from lessons before.

1. down _____   **2.** funny _____

3. jump _____   **4.** fill _____

5. you _____   **6.** tent _____

C. Write each word three times.

1. cast _____ _____ _____

2. fast _____ _____ _____

3. last _____ _____ _____

4. mast _____ _____ _____

5. all _____ _____ _____

6. am _____ _____ _____

Words with -est

best	test	are
nest	west	be

A. Circle your spelling words.

1. Are you my friend?

2. The bird built a nest.

3. Will you be home by five o'clock?

4. The wind came out of the west.

5. She is my best friend.

6. Did you pass the test?

B. Circle the word that is the same as the top one.

west	best	test	nest	are	be
mest	dest	tesf	nost	are	ba
wesf	bost	test	nast	ane	be
wost	bast	tast	nest	ore	de
west	best	tasf	nesf	one	pe

C. Find the missing letters. Then write the word.

1. a _____ _____   _____

2. t e _____ _____   _____

3. n e s _____   _____

Name _____

LESSON 18

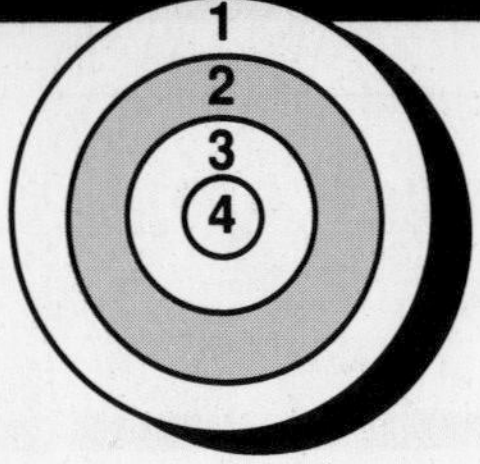

Words with *-est*

best	**test**	**are**
nest	**west**	**be**

A. Fill in the boxes with the right words.

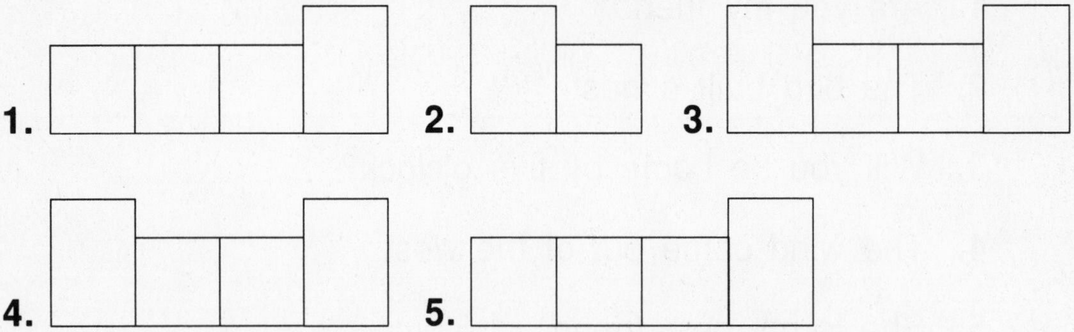

1. 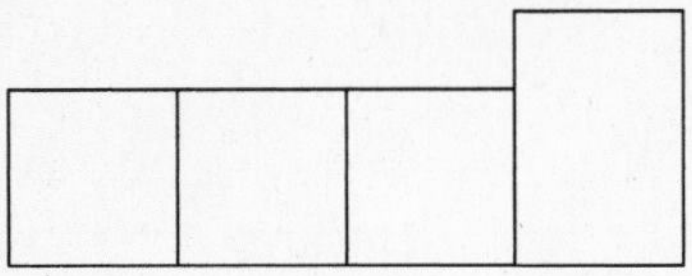

2. 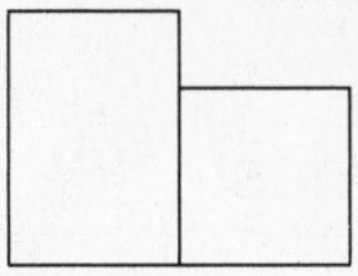

3. 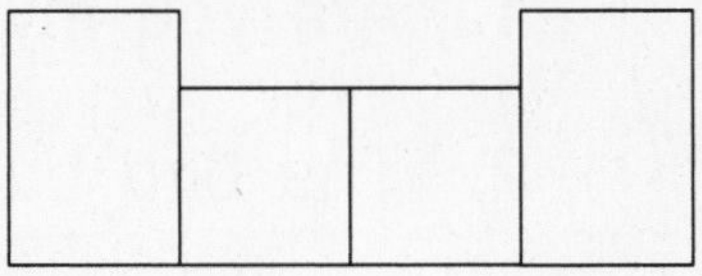

4. 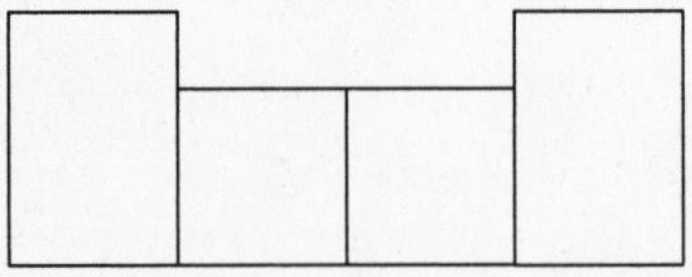

5. 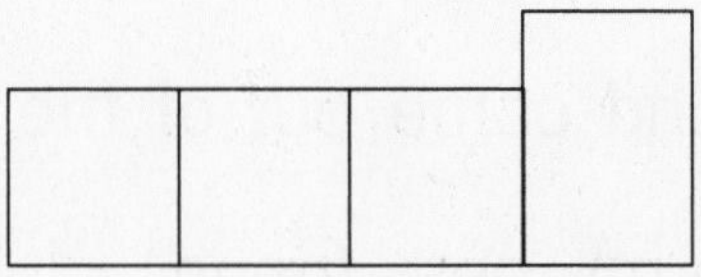

B. Fill in each blank with the right word.

1. The bird built a ____________.
   west nest

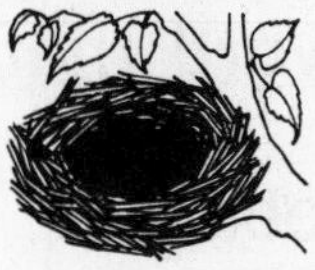

2. Will you ____________ my valentine?
   are be

3. Did you pass the ____________?
   best test

4. The sun sets in the ____________.
   west nest

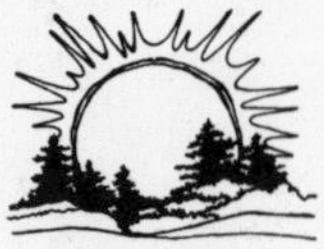

5. They ____________ at school now.
   are be

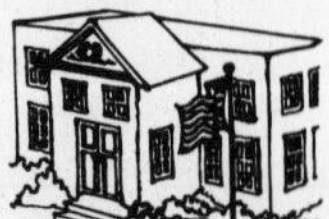

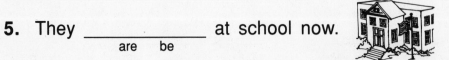

6. You are my ____________ pal.
   best test

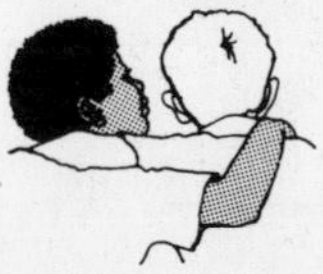

LESSON 18

Words with *-est*

best	test	are
nest	west	be

A. Find the hidden spelling words.

```
e  l  e  t  e  s  t
s  o  b  u  n  g  s
a  r  e  b  e  s  t
s  e  w  e  s  t  u
f  r  o  n  t  s  r
```

B. Fill in each blank with a spelling word.

1. I will _____ glad to take the _____.

2. We will go _____ this summer.

3. You are my _____ friend.

C. Draw a line from the sentence to the right picture.

1. I get this if I am best.
   a.

2. This is a test.
   b.

3. This is a nest.
   c.

4. This is west.
   d.

Words with -est

best	test	are
nest	west	be

A. Write the spelling word that rhymes with the underlined word *and* makes sense.

1. I did my <u>best</u>

And passed the _____.

2. The bird flew <u>west</u>

To find its _____.

B. Write each word three times.

1. best   _____ _____ _____

2. nest   _____ _____ _____

3. test   _____ _____ _____

4. west   _____ _____ _____

5. are   _____ _____ _____

C. Use spelling words to complete the poem.

Baby birds cannot _____ free

Until they pass a _____ ;

They have to learn to flap their wings

And fly out of their _____ .

Words with *-ist* and *-ust*

fist	mist	must
list	dust	rust

A. Circle your spelling words.

1. I took the list to the grocery store.

2. There is mist in fog.

3. I must go home now.

4. There is rust in the pipes.

5. Dust blew in my face.

6. He made a fist with his hand.

B. Circle the word that is the same as the top one.

mist	dust	fist	list	must	rust
wist	dust	fisf	lisf	mast	nust
mist	dusf	fist	list	wust	rnst
misf	bust	tist	tisl	must	rust
msit	bast	first	lost	musf	rusf

C. Find the missing letters. Then write the word.

1. r _____ s t   _____

2. f i _____ _____   _____

3. d u _____ _____   _____

Name _____

Words with *-ist* and *-ust*

fist	mist	must
list	dust	rust

A. Fill in the boxes with the right words.

1.

2.

3.

4.

B. Fill in each blank with the right word.

1. I have a _____ of things to do.
   <u>fist   list</u>

2. There is _____ on my bike.
   <u>rust   must</u>

3. I _____ have an apple to eat!
   <u>rust   must</u>

4. He hit the ball with his _____.
   <u>fist   list</u>

5. Spray the plant with _____.
   <u>mist   dust</u>

6. I need to _____ my room to get it clean.
   <u>mist   dust</u>

Words with *-ist* and *-ust*

fist	mist	must
list	dust	rust

A. Fill in each blank with a spelling word.

1. It is good to make a _____ of things you _____ do.

2. Please _____ your room.

B. Use spelling words to complete the story.

One wet day I was walking in the rain. I came to an old

house. This house _____ be empty, I thought. I looked

in a window. Everything was covered with _____.

There was a car in front. It was spotted with _____.

I felt sad for the empty old house.

C. Draw a line from the sentence to the right picture.

1. I have a list.   a.

2. I use this to dust.   b.

3. This is a fist.   c.

4. This is mist.   d.

Name _____

Words with *-ist* and *-ust*

fist	mist	must
list	dust	rust

A. **Fill in each blank with a spelling word.**

1. She hit the table with her _____.

2. He made a _____ of things to buy.

3. A light rain is called a _____.

4. We _____ eat good foods to stay strong.

5. Tools left in the rain will _____.

6. I use the mop to get rid of _____.

B. **Write these words from lessons before.**

1. bump _____   2. sand _____

3. yellow _____   4. went _____

C. **Write each word three times.**

1. fist   _____   _____   _____

2. list   _____   _____   _____

3. mist   _____   _____   _____

4. dust   _____   _____   _____

5. must   _____   _____   _____

6. rust   _____   _____   _____

Words with *-ter*

batter	bitter	ate
better	butter	but

A. Circle your spelling words.

1. I ate all my food.

2. Do you feel better now?

3. Put some butter on your bread.

4. I want to go, but I can't.

5. The tea tastes bitter.

6. Are you the next batter in the game?

B. Circle the word that is the same as the top one.

butter	ate	batter	better	but	bitter
bntter	afe	baffer	batter	tub	bitter
butter	ate	botter	better	bat	biffer
butten	eat	better	beffer	but	butter
buffer	aet	batter	betten	bnt	bitten

C. Find the missing letters. Then write the word.

1. a _____ e   _____

2. b a t t _____ _____   _____

3. _____ e _____ _____ e r   _____

Name _____

LESSON 20

Words with *-ter*

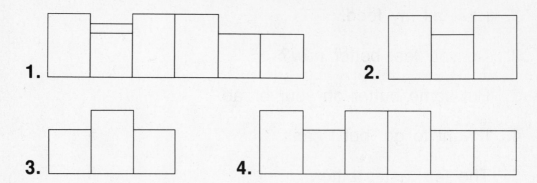

batter	bitter	ate
better	butter	but

A. Fill in the boxes with the right words.

1. ☐☐☐☐☐☐

2. ☐☐☐

3. ☐☐☐

4. ☐☐☐☐☐

B. Fill in each blank with the right word.

1. I feel much _____ .
   butter   better

2. A cake is made from _____ .
   batter   bitter

3. I put _____ on a roll.
   butter   better

4. I _____ a bad apple.
   ate   but

5. Old tea is _____ .
   better   bitter

6. I want to go fishing, _____ I can't.
   ate   but

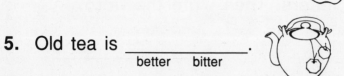

78

Words with -ter

batter	bitter	ate
better	butter	but

A. Find the hidden spelling words.

```
c a s h o u s e
a t b i t t e r
l e g o m a k e
f i s h u k o b
a b a t t e r e
b u t t e r a t
c t r e l o g t
t t a i l o v e
e e r t r e e r
```

B. Use spelling words to complete the story.

I made a lemon cake. But it wasn't very good. I put too

much lemon juice in the _____. It was so

_____! I was sad. But I ate it anyway. A bad cake

is _____ than no cake at all.

C. Write a spelling word under each picture.

1. _____   2. _____   3. _____

Name _____

79

Words with *-ter*

batter	bitter	ate
better	butter	but

A. Use spelling words to complete the puzzle.

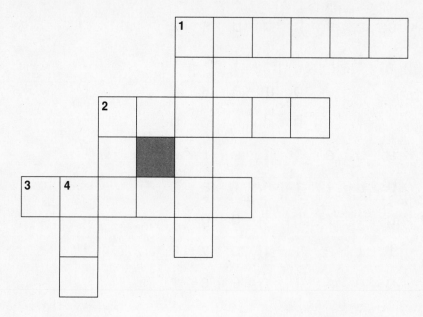

Across

1. bread and _____

2. sour

3. one who bats

Down

1. opposite of worse

2. I want to go, _____ I can't.

4. I _____ the whole pie.

B. Write each word three times.

1. batter _____ _____ _____

2. better _____ _____ _____

3. bitter _____ _____ _____

4. butter _____ _____ _____

belt	melt	eat
felt	on	have

A. Circle your spelling words.

1. The ice is going to melt.

2. I left my belt at home.

3. He has not felt well all day.

4. Do you eat too much?

5. Breakfast is on the table.

6. I have a bad cold.

B. Circle the word that is the same as the top one.

belt	melt	felt	on	eat	have
belt	welt	felf	no	tea	hawe
balt	melf	telf	an	ate	have
belf	melt	felt	en	eat	heva
pelt	welf	fell	on	aet	yave

C. Circle the spelling words that are hidden in the big words. Write the words on the lines.

1. shave _____ 2. gone _____

3. smelt _____ 4. neat _____

LESSON 21   Words with *-elt*

belt	melt	eat
felt	on	have

A. Fill in the boxes with the right words.

1. ☐☐

2. ☐☐☐☐

3. ☐☐☐☐

4. ☐☐☐☐

5. ☐☐☐

B. Fill in each blank with the right word.

1. Did you _____ my orange?
           eat   on

2. A _____ holds up your pants.
      melt   belt

3. I like jelly _____ my toast.
          on   have

4. The ice began to _____.
          felt   melt

5. I do not _____ any money.
        have   on

6. The rabbit's fur _____ soft.
        belt   felt

82

Words with -elt

belt	melt	eat
felt	on	have

A. Find the hidden spelling words.

```
f  e  l  l  o  w  m  a  n
e  a  m  e  f  p  e  x  l
l  t  a  f  b  e  l  u  d
t  h  o  c  e  l  t  u  g
l  a  b  e  l  t  o  n  e
e  v  e  l  k  n  e  i  v
p  e  a  s  p  u  s  h  e
```

B. Find the missing letters. Then write the word.

1. e _____ _____   _____

2. m _____ l t   _____

3. b e _____ _____   _____

C. Draw a line from the picture to the right word.

1.   **a.** belt

2.   **b.** eat

3.   **c.** felt

Name _____

Words with *-elt*

belt	melt	eat
felt	on	have

A. Write the spelling word that rhymes with the underlined word *and* makes sense.

1. I think you are <u>neat</u>,

   So let's go out to _____.

2. Last summer I <u>felt</u>

   That the heat would make me _____.

B. If the picture doesn't fit the word, mark it with an *X*.

belt   melt   felt

C. Use spelling words to complete the story.

One night we were very hungry. We went to

_____ at a restaurant. I ate a huge meal. Now I am

so full I may _____ to take off my _____. I

haven't _____ this bad in a long time.

My friend is ordering dessert. She is putting ice cream

_____ her pie. I wish I hadn't eaten so much dinner!

Words with -*lk*

elk	silk	get
milk	good	into

A. Circle your spelling words.

1. Candy is not good for your teeth.

2. Please get out of the car.

3. Did you drink your milk?

4. The hat was made of silk.

5. An elk is a big animal.

6. She jumped into the pool.

B. Circle the word that is the same as the top one.

silk	elk	milk	good	get	into
sulk	ekl	kilm	goop	teg	into
silk	kel	milk	qood	got	toin
slik	elk	mlik	goob	get	onti
skil	ell	mkil	good	gef	itno

C. Fill in each blank with a spelling word.

1. It is _____ for you to drink _____.

2. She was glad to _____ a _____ dress.

3. An _____ is a big animal.

Name _____

Words with -lk

elk	silk	get
milk	good	into

A. Fill in the boxes with the right words.

1.

2.

3.

4.

B. Fill in each blank with the right word.

1. An _____ is a big animal.
   elk   elf

2. My dress is made of _____.
   milk   silk

3. I did not _____ any milk.
   into   get

4. I hope you have a _____ day.
   good   get

5. Come _____ the house.
   good   into

6. Drink your _____.
   silk   milk

Words with -*lk*

elk	silk	get
milk	good	into

A. Find the missing letters. Then write the word.

1. s ____ ____ ____   _____

2. g ____ ____ d   _____

B. Use spelling words to complete the story.

I was getting ready to go to a party. I put on my new

_____ shirt. Just then, the baby started crying. He

was hungry. I rocked him and gave him some

_____. He started to _____ sleepy. So I put

him _____ the crib. I hope the baby will be

_____ for the sitter.

C. Use spelling words to answer these riddles.

1. You need me for strong and

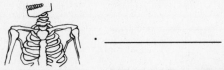 . _____

2. I am made by a , but I become fine

. _____

Name _____

LESSON 22　　**Words with -lk**

elk	silk	get
milk	good	into

A. Draw a line from the word to the right picture.

1. silk

2. elk

3. milk

a.

b.

c.

B. Write these words from lessons before.

1. bitter _____　　2. lock _____

3. melt _____　　4. butter _____

5. sick _____　　6. help _____

C. Write each word three times.

1. elk _____ _____ _____

2. good _____ _____ _____

3. milk _____ _____ _____

4. silk _____ _____ _____

5. get _____ _____ _____

6. into _____ _____ _____

LESSON 23   **Words with -ask**

ask	mask	like
task	do	did

A. **Circle your spelling words.**

1. Put on your new mask.

2. I need to do my spelling.

3. I did the work right.

4. Ask her to go home.

5. A job is called a task.

6. I like you a lot.

B. **Circle the word that is the same as the top one.**

ask	task	mask	do	like	did
aks	fask	mask	da	like	dad
kas	kast	maks	de	kile	ded
ask	tesk	wask	do	lile	dib
sak	task	mosk	bo	liek	did

C. **Find the missing letters. Then write the word.**

1. m _____ _____ k   _____

2. l i _____ _____   _____

3. a _____ _____   _____

Name _____

Words with *-ask*

ask	mask	like
task	do	did

A. Draw a line from the word to the right picture.

1. ask   **a.**

2. task   **b.**

3. mask   **c.**

B. Fill in the boxes with the right words.

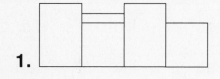

1.   2.   3.

4.   5.   6.

C. Fill in each blank with a spelling word.

1. To hide my face, I wear a _____.

2. Cleaning up my room was a _____.

90

Words with *-ask*

ask	mask	like
task	do	did

A. **Fill in each blank with the right word.**

1. I _____ go home.
   <u>like   did</u>

2. Did she _____ you for a peach?
   <u>task   ask</u>

3. I _____ to eat food.
   <u>task   like</u>

4. How _____ you do?
   <u>ask   do</u>

5. My _____ is to do this work.
   <u>task   ask</u>

6. Take off the _____, and I will see
   <u>like   mask</u>

   your face.

B. **Write these words from lessons before.**

1. into _____   2. silk _____

3. mist _____   4. nest _____

5. are _____   6. fast _____

Name _____   **91**

Words with -ask

ask	mask	like
task	do	did

A. Use spelling words to complete the story.

I like to _____ many things. I _____ to cook, work in the garden, and play sports.

One _____ I don't like is washing dishes. I think I'll _____ my friend to wash them. Maybe we could make a deal. I could cook, and she could wash the dishes.

B. Fill in each blank with a spelling word.

1. _____ she _____ you to her party?

2. I _____ not like this _____.

3. Will you wear a _____ to hide your face?

C. Write each word three times.

1. ask   _____   _____   _____

2. task   _____   _____   _____

3. mask   _____   _____   _____

4. do   _____   _____   _____

5. like   _____   _____   _____

6. did   _____   _____   _____

Words with *-ten*

mitten	written	new
kitten	our	out

A. Circle your spelling words.

1. We live in our house.

2. Is that dress new?

3. Have you been out today?

4. A small cat is a kitten.

5. Put the mitten on my hand.

6. The report was neatly written.

B. Circle the word that is the same as the top one.

new	out	our	written	kitten	mitten
now	ouf	ruo	wridten	kettin	witten
wen	out	our	written	kiffen	mitter
naw	tou	oun	writtin	kitten	mitten
new	tuo	uor	writter	kitter	miffen

C. Fill in each blank with a spelling word.

1. Was the story _____ by that girl?

2. Have you been to _____ house?

3. Is that a _____ dress?

Name _____

LESSON 24

Words with *-ten*

mitten	written	new
kitten	our	out

A. Fill in the boxes with the right words.

1.

2.

3.

4.

B. Fill in each blank with the right word.

1. A little cat is a _____.
   <u>written   kitten</u>

2. This is _____ house.
   <u>out   our</u>

3. I lost one _____.
   <u>mitten   written</u>

4. Put the cat _____ now!
   <u>out   new</u>

5. It was _____ in pencil.
   <u>written   mitten</u>

6. Do you have a _____ dress?
   <u>out   new</u>

94

Words with *-ten*

mitten	written	new
kitten	our	out

A. **Find the hidden spelling words.**

```
s a f l a m i n g o s
l b l o w i s i o u r
n d w r i t t e n t c
e o w e a t h a v e h
a g o a t e a r i c e
t r a i n n e w c o w
s l i c k i t t e n s
t r r e a v e s l o w
p e r s o c b m o w e
l a w o w c a r t i v
```

B. **Find the missing letters. Then write the word.**

1. o _____ t   _____

2. n _____ _____   _____

C. **Use spelling words to complete the story.**

I took my _____ off. I showed my friend where

our _____ had scratched me. The kitten is

_____. It doesn't like to stay _____ of the

house at night. But it will be outside tonight!

Name _____

Words with *-ten*

mitten	written	new
kitten	our	out

A. Draw a line from the word to the right picture.

1. written

a.

2. mitten

b.

3. kitten

c.

B. Write these words from the last lesson.

1. ask _____   2. mask _____

3. like _____   4. do _____

5. did _____   6. task _____

C. Write each word three times.

1. written _____ _____ _____

2. kitten _____ _____ _____

3. mitten _____ _____ _____

4. out _____ _____ _____

5. new _____ _____ _____

6. our _____ _____ _____

96

Words with *-ond*

bond	pond	ran
fond	please	ride

A. Circle your spelling words.

1. The duck is in the pond.

2. Please help me.

3. I am very fond of her.

4. We ran all the way home.

5. Do you want to ride my bike?

6. Things that stick together form a bond.

B. Circle the word that is the same as the top one.

bond	fond	pond	please	ran	ride
band	tond	pond	qlease	ran	ride
dond	fond	dond	please	rau	ribe
bond	fonb	pand	plaese	nar	nide
bonb	foud	poud	blease	ren	edir

C. Finish the sentences.

1. Please get me _____.

2. Do you ride _____?

Name _____

Words with -ond

bond	pond	ran
fond	please	ride

A. Fill in the boxes with the right words.

1.

2.

3.

4.

B. Fill in each blank with the right word.

1. Glue will _____ things together.
   <u>fond   bond</u>

2. My dog _____ away.
   <u>ran   ride</u>

3. I am very _____ of you.
   <u>bond   fond</u>

4. The ducks are in the _____.
   <u>pond   bond</u>

5. Let's _____ in the car.
   <u>ran   ride</u>

6. _____ get me that pen.
   <u>Pond   Please</u>

98

Words with *-ond*

bond	pond	ran
fond	please	ride

A. Find the hidden spelling words.

```
s  c  a  t  f  i  s  h  a  n  d
o  n  e  t  o  n  a  e  w  o  u
c  o  b  o  n  d  g  r  a  s  s
k  p  o  n  d  p  e  a  n  e  t
b  a  t  w  o  l  o  n  g  e  t
i  s  c  a  r  e  b  o  a  t  s
s  o  n  g  r  a  s  p  l  a  t
o  n  o  t  e  s  a  e  a  t  s
d  x  r  i  d  e  t  s  t  a  b
b  c  i  d  a  r  l  u  m  e  n
```

B. Find the missing letters. Then write the word.

1. p l _____ _____ _____ e   _____

2. r _____ d _____   _____

C. Fill in each blank with a spelling word.

1. I try to _____ my parents.

2. Are you _____ of apples?

3. Let's _____ the bumper cars.

4. We can fish in the _____.

Name _____

© 1991 Steck-Vaughn Company. Target 180

Words with *-ond*

bond	pond	ran
fond	please	ride

A. Draw a line from the word to the right picture.

1. pond

a.

2. bond

b.

3. ride

c.

B. Write these words from the last lesson.

1. written _____   **2.** kitten _____

3. mitten _____   **4.** new _____

5. our _____   **6.** out _____

C. Use spelling words to complete the story.

If you are friends with someone, it means you have a

special _____. Many friends like the same things.

They may like to _____ bikes in the country. Or

perhaps they like to fish in a _____. Friends also like

to _____ each other. One of my best friends gave me

a surprise party.

Words with *-ap*

clap	trap	no
slap	wrap	now

A. Circle your spelling words.

1. Please wrap my present.

2. I had to say no to him.

3. Can you clap your hands?

4. Come to see me now.

5. He set a trap for the mouse.

6. Do not slap at the bees.

B. Circle the word that is the same as the top one.

clap	slap	trap	wrap	no	now
claq	pals	tnap	wrop	on	nom
clap	slop	traq	wrap	mo	now
calp	slap	trap	wnap	no	won

C. Use spelling words to complete the story.

The trapdoor spider is smart. Its home is a _____.

The spider waits in its hole. The hole is covered with silk.

When the spider feels a bug walk above, it will _____

the bug into the hole. Then it will _____ the bug up

and eat it later.

Name _____

LESSON 26   Words with *-ap*

clap	trap	no
slap	wrap	now

A. Fill in the boxes with the right words.

1.
2.
3.
4.
5.

B. Fill in each blank with the right word.

1. Do not _____ at the bees.
   wrap   slap

2. You can _____ your hands.
   wrap   clap

3. Let's do our work _____.
   no   now

4. Did you _____ my gift?
   trap   wrap

5. We set a _____ for the mouse.
   trap   wrap

6. I say yes, but you say _____.
   no   now

102

Words with *-ap*

clap	trap	no
slap	wrap	now

A. Find the hidden spelling words.

```
b  i  g  f  i  s  h  f  i  n  d
o  n  o  w  a  l  a  n  d  w  a
a  o  a  r  s  a  t  e  a  r  n
t  r  a  p  x  p  l  u  m  a  d
r  i  c  h  u  p  h  a  p  p  y
a  b  c  d  e  f  g  h  i  j  k
m  a  p  c  l  a  p  u  s  h  s
p  i  g  c  o  w  h  o  r  s  e
```

B. Find the missing letters. Then write the word.

1. t r _____ _____ _____

2. w _____ _____ p _____

C. Fill in each blank with a spelling word.

1. To show that we like a play, we _____.

2. A blow with the open hand is a _____.

3. The hunter set a _____ for the bear.

4. I forgot to _____ your present.

5. The sign said "Do It _____."

Name _____

103

Words with *-ap*

clap	trap	no
slap	wrap	now

A. Draw a line from the word to the right picture.

1. clap

a.

2. slap

b.

3. trap

c.

B. Write these words from the last lesson.

1. bond _____ 2. fond _____

3. pond _____ 4. please _____

5. ride _____ 6. ran _____

C. Write each word three times.

1. clap _____ _____ _____

2. slap _____ _____ _____

3. trap _____ _____ _____

4. wrap _____ _____ _____

5. no _____ _____ _____

6. now _____ _____ _____

Words with *-ick*

click	flick	so
brick	slick	she

A. Circle your spelling words.

1. She is my sister.

2. My house is made of brick.

3. Ice can make roads slick.

4. Let's go so we can see it.

5. A camera goes "click."

6. Flick the bug off my arm, please!

B. Circle the word that is the same as the top one.

click	brick	flick	slick	she	so
clich	drick	tlick	slick	sbe	sa
click	bnick	flich	slich	she	se
cliok	brick	fliok	sliok	hes	so
klick	brich	flick	alick	seh	os

C. Write a spelling word under each picture.

1. _____   **2.** _____   **3.** _____

Name _____

Words with *-ick*

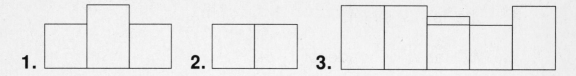

| click | flick | so |
| brick | slick | she |

A. Fill in the boxes with the right words.

1. 2. 3.

B. Find the missing letters. Then write the word.

1. c l _____ _____ _____   _____

2. _____ h e   _____

3. f _____ i _____ _____   _____

C. Use spelling words to complete the story.

    I saw a show last night. It was _____ good! The show was about a little girl and a dog from Kansas. A bad storm blew them to the Land of Oz. They went on a Yellow _____ Road. They wanted to get back to Kansas. The girl had to _____ her heels three times. When she opened her eyes, she was back home.

D. Circle the letters that are the same in each word.

       click   flick   brick   slick

The word family is _____.

Words with *-ick*

| click | flick | so |
| brick | slick | she |

A. Find the hidden spelling words.

```
b  r  i  c  k  s  o  m  e
g  a  f  l  i  c  k  i  t
u  s  l  i  c  k  a  n  d
e  h  o  c  e  s  t  a  r
s  e  r  k  r  a  m  e  r
t  a  e  s  t  e  e  r  s
w  r  a  c  p  b  a  n  d
```

B. Fill in each blank with the right word.

1. My house is made of _____.
   <small>click   brick</small>

2. The ice made the road _____.
   <small>slick   flick</small>

3. The camera goes "_____."
   <small>slick   click</small>

4. _____ is a smart girl.
   <small>Slick   She</small>

5. Will you _____ off the light
   <small>click   flick</small>

   switch?

Name _____

Words with -ick

click	flick	so
brick	slick	she

A. Use spelling words to complete the puzzle.

Across

1. She's _____ nice.

2. _____ on the light.

3. red stone used for building

Down

1. Ice makes roads _____.

4. the sound a camera makes

B. Write each word three times.

1. click _____ _____ _____

2. so _____ _____ _____

3. brick _____ _____ _____

4. she _____ _____ _____

5. flick _____ _____ _____

6. slick _____ _____ _____

Words with -ing

cling	fling	soon
bring	sting	that

A. Circle your spelling words.

1. A bee can sting you.

2. I will be home soon.

3. Wet clothes cling to you.

4. Don't fling your clothes down.

5. Please bring my coat to me.

6. That is a funny joke.

B. Circle the word that is the same as the top one.

bring	sting	fling	cling	soon	that
dring	sfing	fling	cliug	sone	thaf
bring	stirg	fliny	clinq	soou	tnat
bning	sting	fliug	cling	noos	that
brinq	stinq	tling	glinc	soon	thot

C. Write these words from lessons before.

1. please _____   2. wrap _____

3. brick _____   4. pond _____

5. clap _____   6. flick _____

Name _____

LESSON 28

Words with *-ing*

cling	fling	soon
bring	sting	that

A. Fill in each blank with the right word.

1. Bees can _____ you.
   cling   sting

2. Please _____ me my hat.
   bring   cling

3. You can _____ a Frisbee.
   sting   fling

4. A baby will _____ to its mother.
   cling   bring

5. I will be home _____.
   that   soon
   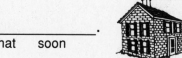

B. Fill in the boxes with the right words.

1.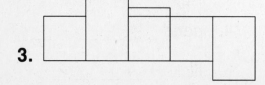

2.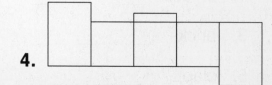

3.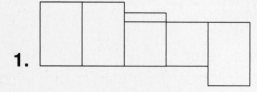

4.

110

LESSON 28

Words with *-ing*

cling	fling	soon
bring	sting	that

A. Find the hidden spelling words.

```
c h o w b r i n g
l a m i c r e a m
c r e n l t h a t
h d l g i n g e r
e f l i n g l e t
s t i n g l o v e
s o o n o t w a r
```

B. Fill in each blank with a spelling word.

1. I will be there _____.

2. Did you _____ a Frisbee?

3. Did that bee _____ your arm?

C. Use spelling words to answer these riddles.

1. It sounds like fling, and do it. _____

2. It means it won't be long and sounds

   like  . _____

© 1991 Steck-Vaughn Company. Target 180

Name _____

111

Words with *-ing*

cling	fling	soon
bring	sting	that

A. Find the missing letters. Then write the word.

1. s _____ _____ n   _____

2. t h _____ _____   _____

B. Use spelling words to complete the story.

I went to our school picnic. It was my turn to _____

flowers and drinks. I picked some red flowers on the way to

school. I _____ found out that was not smart.

There were some bees in the flowers. They began to fly

out and _____ anyone who was close. All my friends

began to run. My teacher shook her head and said to bring

something safe next time. _____ was the last time I

brought flowers to a party.

C. Write each word three times.

1. fling   _____ _____ _____

2. bring   _____ _____ _____

3. sting   _____ _____ _____

4. cling   _____ _____ _____

slim	trim	this
skim	brim	they

A. Circle your spelling words.

1. I can trim the paper.

2. Slim people are not fat.

3. I like skim milk.

4. The cup is filled to its brim.

5. They are my friends.

6. Is this your pencil?

B. Circle the word that is the same as the top one.

slim	skim	trim	brim	this	they
slim	shim	frim	drim	that	thay
slin	shin	triw	bnim	this	thag
sliw	skin	tnim	brim	tkis	they
slem	skim	trim	briw	fhis	thoy

C. Finish the sentences.

1. Please <u>trim</u> the _____.

2. The cup's <u>brim</u> is _____.

3. <u>They</u> went to the _____.

Words with -im

slim	trim	this
skim	brim	they

A. Fill in the boxes with the right words.

1.

2.

3.

4.

B. Fill in each blank with the right word.

1. I drink _____ milk.
   <small>skim   trim</small>

2. _____ are going home.
   <small>This   They</small>

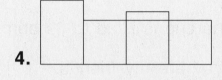

3. Can you _____ my hair?
   <small>skim   trim</small>

4. Is _____ your pencil?
   <small>this   they</small>

5. The cup is filled to its _____.
   <small>slim   brim</small>

6. Are you _____ and trim?
   <small>brim   slim</small>

LESSON 29

Words with *-im*

slim	trim	this
skim	brim	they

A. Find the hidden spelling words.

```
f  i  v  e  s  e  v  e  n  s
c  a  r  m  y  b  e  a  n  s
a  o  u  s  t  h  i  s  l  i
n  p  a  k  f  l  o  b  t  x
t  t  r  i  m  e  a  r  d  a
a  e  t  m  e  b  h  i  s  n
k  c  h  i  s  l  i  m  o  d
e  s  e  t  u  p  p  o  t  o
s  b  y  t  h  e  s  n  o  f
```

B. Find the missing letters. Then write the word.

1. t h _____ s   _____

2. s l _____ _____   _____

3. b _____ _____ m   _____

C. Fill in each blank with a spelling word.

1. I have read _____ book.

2. We will _____ the Christmas tree.

3. A hat has a _____.

Name _____

115

Words with *-im*

slim	trim	this
skim	brim	they

A. Draw a line from the word to the right picture.

1. brim

a.

2. skim

b.

3. slim

c.

B. Use spelling words to complete the story.

Many people pay attention to their health. They try to stay

_____. They watch what they eat. They

_____ the fat off meat and drink _____ milk.

Getting exercise is important, too. Some people take a

walk every day. They feel that the fresh air is good for them.

C. Write each word three times.

1. slim _____ _____ _____

2. brim _____ _____ _____

3. skim _____ _____ _____

4. trim _____ _____ _____

Words with -op

crop	prop	was
drop	stop	any

A. Circle your spelling words.

1. Please don't drop my milk.

2. The car came to a stop.

3. Prop up my pillow, please.

4. I was at home all day.

5. Do you want any bread?

6. Corn is a crop that farmers grow.

B. Circle the word that is the same as the top one.

drop	crop	any	prop	stop	was
prod	cnop	auy	grop	shop	saw
drop	enop	ang	pnop	sfop	was
brop	crop	aug	prop	stap	wos
droq	crep	any	prap	stop	mas

C. Write these words from the last lesson.

1. slim _____

2. skim _____

3. trim _____

4. brim _____

5. this _____

6. they _____

Name _____

Words with *-op*

crop	prop	was
drop	stop	any

A. Fill in the boxes with the right words.

1.
2.
3.
4.

B. Fill in each blank with the right word.

1. He _____ very good today.
   <small>well   was</small>
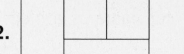

2. Do not _____ the baby!
   <small>any   drop</small>
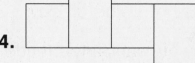

3. Please _____ up my pillow.
   <small>crop   prop</small>
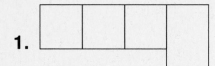

4. Did you want _____ water?
   <small>was   any</small>

5. We had a good _____ of corn.
   <small>crop   stop</small>

6. The car could not _____ in time.
   <small>drop   stop</small>

Words with -op

crop	prop	was
drop	stop	any

A. Find the hidden spelling words.

```
p a r t y l a t e
d r o p e b p w n
a s k e s u r e e
n m a s k m o l a
y c a s t o p l t
e n e s t s t e w
o c r o p t a r s
n w a s s l o w o
```

B. Find the missing letters. Then write the word.

1. w _____ _____   _____

2. p _____ o _____   _____

3. d r _____ _____   _____

C. Fill in each blank with a spelling word.

1. I don't eat _____ junk food.

2. Put one _____ of this on the cut.

3. We had a big _____ of wheat.

4. She _____ on time.

Name _____   **119**

Words with *-op*

crop	prop	was
drop	stop	any

A. Draw a line from the word to the right picture.

1. crop

a.

2. stop

b.

3. drop

c.

B. Fill in each blank with a spelling word.

1. Did you _____ your books?

2. He did not _____ at the corner.

3. Are there _____ apples in that basket?

C. Use spelling words to complete the story.

Jack and his mother did not have _____ money. So Jack went to sell their cow. He traded the cow for some beans. Jack's mother was not happy with him.

But a surprising thing happened. They planted the beans. The beans did not _____ growing.

"What a _____ of beans we will have!" cried Jack.

My Word List

Words I Can Spell

Put a ✓ in the box beside each word you spell correctly on your weekly test.

1

☐ a   ☐ at

☐ as   ☐ can

☐ an   ☐ away

2

☐ bad   ☐ sad

☐ mad   ☐ come

☐ dad   ☐ down

3

☐ bag   ☐ wag

☐ rag   ☐ find

☐ tag   ☐ funny

4

☐ pen   ☐ big

☐ ten   ☐ he

☐ hen   ☐ blue

5

☐ jet   ☐ wet

☐ net   ☐ help

☐ pet   ☐ here

Words To Review

If you miss a word on your test, write it here. Practice it until you can spell it correctly. Then check the box beside the word.

_____

_____

_____

_____

_____

_____

_____

_____

_____

_____

_____

_____

Name _____

My Word List

Words I Can Spell

Put a ✓ in the box beside each word you spell correctly on your weekly test.

6

☐ pack ☐ tack

☐ rack ☐ jump

☐ sack ☐ little

7

☐ kick ☐ tick

☐ pick ☐ look

☐ sick ☐ make

8

☐ bell ☐ well

☐ sell ☐ me

☐ tell ☐ my

9

☐ ill ☐ pill

☐ fill ☐ not

☐ hill ☐ one

10

☐ rock ☐ lock

☐ sock ☐ play

☐ dock ☐ red

Words To Review

If you miss a word on your test, write it here. Practice it until you can spell it correctly. Then check the box beside the word.

_____

_____

_____

_____

_____

_____

_____

_____

_____

_____

_____

_____

_____

_____

_____

My Word List

Words I Can Spell

Put a ✓ in the box beside each word you spell correctly on your weekly test.

11

☐ mess ☐ run

☐ less ☐ said

☐ came ☐ see

12

☐ camp ☐ ramp

☐ damp ☐ you

☐ lamp ☐ we

13

☐ bump ☐ dump

☐ lump ☐ three

☐ pump ☐ two

14

☐ band ☐ hand

☐ land ☐ for

☐ sand ☐ go

15

☐ mend ☐ lend

☐ bend ☐ where

☐ send ☐ yellow

Words To Review

If you miss a word on your test, write it here. Practice it until you can spell it correctly. Then check the box beside the word.

_____

_____

_____

_____

_____

_____

_____

_____

_____

_____

_____

_____

_____

Name _____

My Word List

Words I Can Spell

Put a ✓ in the box beside each word you spell correctly on your weekly test.

16

☐ dent   ☐ went

☐ sent   ☐ to

☐ tent   ☐ up

17

☐ cast   ☐ mast

☐ fast   ☐ all

☐ last   ☐ am

18

☐ best   ☐ west

☐ nest   ☐ are

☐ test   ☐ be

19

☐ fist   ☐ dust

☐ list   ☐ must

☐ mist   ☐ rust

20

☐ batter   ☐ butter

☐ better   ☐ ate

☐ bitter   ☐ but

Words To Review

If you miss a word on your test, write it here. Practice it until you can spell it correctly. Then check the box beside the word.

_____

_____

_____

_____

_____

_____

_____

_____

_____

_____

_____

_____

_____

My Word List

Words I Can Spell

Put a ✓ in the box beside each word you spell correctly on your weekly test.

21

☐ belt   ☐ on

☐ felt   ☐ eat

☐ melt   ☐ have

22

☐ elk   ☐ good

☐ milk   ☐ get

☐ silk   ☐ into

23

☐ ask   ☐ do

☐ task   ☐ like

☐ mask   ☐ did

24

☐ mitten   ☐ our

☐ kitten   ☐ new

☐ written   ☐ out

25

☐ bond   ☐ please

☐ fond   ☐ ran

☐ pond   ☐ ride

Words To Review

If you miss a word on your test, write it here. Practice it until you can spell it correctly. Then check the box beside the word.

_____

_____

_____

_____

_____

_____

_____

_____

_____

_____

_____

_____

_____

_____

Name _____

© 1991 Steck-Vaughn Company. Target 180

My Word List

Words I Can Spell

Put a ✓ in the box beside each word you spell correctly on your weekly test.

26

☐ clap ☐ wrap

☐ slap ☐ no

☐ trap ☐ now

27

☐ click ☐ slick

☐ brick ☐ so

☐ flick ☐ she

28

☐ cling ☐ sting

☐ bring ☐ soon

☐ fling ☐ that

29

☐ slim ☐ brim

☐ skim ☐ this

☐ trim ☐ they

30

☐ crop ☐ stop

☐ drop ☐ was

☐ prop ☐ any

Words To Review

If you miss a word on your test, write it here. Practice it until you can spell it correctly. Then check the box beside the word.

_____

_____

_____

_____

_____

_____

_____

_____

_____

_____

_____

_____